The Grandeur of

GOD

The Grandeur of

GOD

Selections from Two Thousand Years of Catholic Spiritual Writing

✳

EDITED BY JOSEPH DUREPOS

Compiled by Teresa de Bertodano

LOYOLAPRESS.

CHICAGO

LOYOLAPRESS.

3441 N. ASHLAND AVENUE
CHICAGO, ILLINOIS 60657
(800) 621-1008
WWW.LOYOLABOOKS.ORG

The majority of the material used in this collection is taken from *The Book of Catholic Wisdom: 2000 Years of Spiritual Writing* © 1999 Teresa de Bertodano. All rights reserved. *The Book of Catholic Wisdom* was first published in 1999 by Darton, Longman and Todd, Ltd., London, U.K. The first North American edition was published in hardcover by Loyola Press in 2001.

The Scripture quotations contained herein are from the New Revised Standard Version Bible: Catholic Edition, copyright © 1993 and 1989 by the Division of Christian Education of the National Council of the Churches of Christ in the U.S.A. Used by permission. All rights reserved.

Jacket design by Rick Franklin
Jacket illustration by Kathryn Seckman
Interior design by Adam Moroschan

Library of Congress Cataloging-in-Publication Data
The grandeur of God : selections from two thousand years of Catholic spiritual writing
/ edited by Joseph Durepos ; compiled by Teresa de Bertodano.
     p.   cm.
     ISBN 0-8294-2132-7
  1. Christian life—Catholic authors. 2. Spirituality—Catholic Church. I.
Durepos, Joseph, 1955– II. De Bertodano, Teresa.
BV4501.3.G735 2005
248.4'82—dc22

                                       2004021357

Printed in the United States of America
05 06 07 08 09 10 Bang 10 9 8 7 6 5 4 3 2 1

"The world is charged
with the grandeur of God."

GERARD MANLEY HOPKINS

Contents

Contents

Contents

Contents

Contents

Contents

Contents

Contents

A Note to the Reader

I put some strict editorial constraints on myself when preparing this book. My task was to select readings that would give you a sense of the depth, beauty, and richness of Catholic spiritual writing. I decided to limit myself to one hundred readings, and I also tried to keep the readings relatively brief. Obviously, this meant that I had to leave out more great writing than could possibly be included. It also limited what this book can accomplish. It is a humble invitation. I hope it will be your starting point on a journey into the great splendor of Catholic writing.

But these constraints also had their advantages. Since I didn't have to be comprehensive, I could be highly selective. From the vast library of two thousand years of Catholic writing, I was able to pick some of the most succinct and memorable passages. I preferred those that I thought spoke most directly to modern readers and those that address matters that we need to hear about now. The rules also permitted me to pick some readings simply because I like them.

The readings begin with St. Paul and proceed chronologically to Pope John Paul II and other writers of the present. My choices are weighted toward more recent centuries (though all eras of the church are represented), and a discerning eye will detect a liking for Jesuits and others inspired by Ignatian spirituality. All these readings have been tested by time. They are classics. They speak from the heart of the church. They all resonate with the truth expressed famously by the great Jesuit poet Gerard Manley Hopkins, "The world is charged with the grandeur of God." This sacramental, Catholic vision sees God in all things. I hope you will find God in these pages.

—JOSEPH DUREPOS

The Grandeur of God

I

Jesus Christ Is Lord
(PHILIPPIANS 2:1–11)

I f then there is any encouragement in Christ, any consolation from love, any sharing in the Spirit, any compassion and sympathy, make my joy complete: be of the same mind, having the same love, being in full accord and of one mind. Do nothing from selfish ambition or conceit, but in humility regard others as better than yourselves. Let each of you look not to your own interests, but to the interests of others. Let the same mind be in you that was in Christ Jesus,

> who, though he was in the form of God,
>> did not regard equality with God
>> as something to be exploited,
>> but emptied himself,

taking the form of a slave,

being born in human likeness.

And being found in human form,

he humbled himself

and became obedient to the point of death—

even death on a cross.

Therefore God also highly exalted him

and gave him the name

that is above every name,

so that at the name of Jesus

every knee should bend,

in heaven and on earth and under the earth,

and every tongue should confess

that Jesus Christ is Lord,

to the glory of God the Father.

✳ ST. PAUL (CA. 10–CA. 67)

2

Nothing Can Separate Us from the Love of God

(ROMANS 8:38–39)

For I am convinced that neither death,

nor life,

nor angels,

nor rulers,

nor things present,

nor things to come,

nor powers,

nor height,

nor depth,

nor anything else in all creation,

will be able to separate us from the love of God

   in Christ Jesus our Lord.

✳ ST. PAUL (CA. 10–CA. 67)

3
Halcyon Days

The halcyon is a seabird that nests by the shore, laying its eggs in the sand, and bringing forth its young in the middle of winter when the sea beats against the land in violent and frequent storms. But during the seven days while the halcyon broods—for it takes but seven days to hatch its young—all winds sink to rest, and the sea grows calm. And as it then is in need of food for its young ones, the most bountiful God grants this little creature another seven days of calm: that it may feed its young. Since all sailors know of this, they give this time the name of the *halcyon days*.

These things are ordered by the Providence of God for the creatures that are without reason, that you may be led to seek of God the things you need for your salvation.

And when for this small bird he holds back the great and fearful sea, and bids it be calm in winter, what will he not do for you made in his own image? And if he should so tenderly cherish the halcyon, how much more will he not give you, when you call upon him with all your heart?

✳ ST. BASIL THE GREAT (CA. 330–79)

4

Honor Christ with Golden Hearts

Would you honor the body of Christ? Do not despise his nakedness; do not honor him here in church clothed in silk vestments and then pass him by unclothed and frozen outside. Remember that he who said, "This is my body," and made good his words, also said, "You saw me hungry and gave me no food," and, "in so far as you did it not to one of these, you did it not to me." In the first sense the body of Christ does not need clothing but worship from a pure heart. In the second sense it does need clothing and all the care we can give it.

We must learn to be discerning Christians and to honor Christ in the way in which he wants to be honored. It is only right that honor given to anyone should take the form most acceptable to the recipient, not to the giver. Peter thought he was honoring the Lord when he tried to stop him washing his feet, but this was far from being genuine homage. So give God the honor he asks for, that is, give your money generously to the poor. God has no need of golden vessels but of golden hearts.

I am not saying you should not give golden altar vessels and so on, but I am insisting that nothing can take the place of almsgiving. The Lord will not refuse to accept the first kind of gift, but he prefers the second, and quite naturally, because in the first case only the donor benefits, in the second case the poor get the benefit. The gift of a chalice may be ostentatious; almsgiving is pure benevolence.

✳ St. John Chrysostom (ca. 349–407)

5

Christic in the Poor

What is the use of loading Christ's table with gold cups while he himself is starving? Feed the hungry, and then if you have any money left over, spend it on the altar table. Will you make a cup of gold and withhold a cup of water? What use is it to adorn the altar with cloth of gold hangings and deny Christ a coat for his back! What would that profit you? Tell me: if you saw someone starving and refused to give him any food but instead spent your money on adorning the altar with gold, would he thank you? Would he not rather be outraged? Or if you saw someone in rags and stiff with cold and then did not give him clothing but set up golden columns in his honor, would he not say he was being made a fool of and insulted?

Consider that Christ is that tramp who comes in need of a night's lodging. You turn him away and then start laying rugs on the floor, draping the walls, hanging lamps on silver chains on the columns. Meanwhile the tramp is locked up in prison, and you never give him a glance. Well, again, I am not condemning munificence in these matters. Make your house beautiful by all means but also look after the poor, or rather look after the poor first. No one was ever condemned for not adorning his house, but those who neglect the poor were threatened with hellfire for all eternity and a life of torment with devils. Adorn your house if you will, but do not forget your brother in distress. He is a temple of infinitely greater value.

✳ ST. JOHN CHRYSOSTOM (CA. 349–407)

6

Love Your Neighbor

You do not yet see God, but by loving your neighbor you gain the sight of God; by loving your neighbor you purify your eye for seeing God, as John says clearly: "If you do not love the brother whom you see, how will you be able to love God whom you do not see?"

You are told: love God. If you say to me: "Show me the one I am to love," what shall I answer, except what John himself says: "No one has ever seen God"? Do not think that you are altogether unsuited to seeing God— no, for John states: "God is love, and he who dwells in love is dwelling in God." Love your neighbor therefore, and observe the source of that love in you; there, as best you can, you will see God.

So then, begin to love your neighbor. "Share your bread with the hungry, and bring the homeless poor into your house; if you see the naked, cover him, and do not despise the servants of your kinsfolk."

If you do this, what will you obtain? "Then shall your light break forth like the morning." Your light is your God; to you he is "morning light," because he will come to you after the night of the world; he neither rises nor sets, because he abides always.

By loving your neighbor and being concerned about your neighbor, you make progress on your journey. Where is your journey, if not to the Lord God, to him whom we must love with all our heart, and with all our soul, and with all our mind? We have not yet reached the Lord, but we have our neighbor with us. So then, support him with whom you are traveling so that you may come to him with whom you long to dwell.

✳ AUGUSTINE OF HIPPO (354–430)

7

Late Have I Loved You

Late have I loved you, Beauty so ancient and so new,
late have I loved you!
Lo, you were within,
but I outside, seeking there for you,
and upon the shapely things you have made I rushed
   headlong,
I, misshapen.
You were with me, but I was not with you.
They held me back far from you,
those things which would have no being
were they not in you.
You called, shouted, broke through my deafness;
you flared, blazed, banished my blindness;

you lavished your fragrance, I gasped, and now I pant
   for you;
I tasted you, and I hunger and thirst;
you touched me, and I burned for your peace.

✳ AUGUSTINE OF HIPPO (354–430)

8

St. Patrick's Breastplate

Christ with me, Christ before me,

Christ behind me, Christ within me,

Christ beneath me, Christ above me,

Christ at my right, Christ at my left,

Christ in my lying down, Christ in my sitting,

Christ in my arising.

Christ in the heart of everyone who thinks of me,

Christ in the mouth of everyone who speaks to me,

Christ in every eye that sees me,

Christ in every ear that hears me.

✳ ST. PATRICK (CA. 390–CA. 461)

9
Two Kinds of Mercy

There are two kinds of mercy then, mercy on earth and mercy in heaven, human mercy and divine mercy. What is human mercy like? It makes you concerned for the hardship of the poor. What is divine mercy like? It forgives sinners. Whatever generosity human mercy shows during our life on earth, divine mercy repays when we reach our fatherland. In this world God is cold and hungry in all the poor, as he himself said: "As you did it to one of the least of these my brethren, you did it to me." God then is pleased to give from heaven, but he desires to receive on earth.

✳ CAESARIUS OF ARLES (CA. 470–542)

IO

Believing in the Invisible

Who then is God? He is Father, Son, and Holy Spirit, one God. Seek no further concerning God, for those who wish to know the great deep must first review the natural world. For knowledge of the Trinity is properly likened to the depths of the sea, according to that saying of the Sage. And the great deep, who shall fathom it? Since, just as the depth of the sea is invisible to human sight, even so the godhead of the Trinity is found to be unknowable by human senses. And thus if, I say, a man wishes to know what he ought to believe, let him not think that he understands better by speech than by believing; because when he seeks it, knowledge of the godhead will recede farther than it was.

Therefore seek the supreme wisdom, not by verbal debate, but by the perfection of a good life, not with the tongue, but with the faith that issues from singleness of heart, not with that which is gathered from the guests of a learned irreligion. If then you seek the unutterable by discussion, he will fly farther from you than he was. If you seek by faith, Wisdom shall stand in her accustomed station at the gate, and where she dwells she shall at least in part be seen. But then is she also truly in some measure attained when the invisible is believed in a manner that passes understanding, for God must be believed invisible as he is, though he be partly seen by the pure heart.

✳ COLUMBANUS (CA. 543–615)

II

The Cross Is the Glory of Christ

The cross is called the glory of Christ, and his exaltation; it is the chalice for which he longed, the consummation of his sufferings on our behalf. It is the glory of Christ—listen to his words: "Now is the Son of man glorified, and God is glorified in him, and God will glorify him at once." And again: "Glorify me, Father, with the glory that I had with you before the world was made." And again: "Father, glorify your name. So there came a voice from the heavens: I have glorified it, and I will glorify it again." By this he means the glory that Christ received on the cross.

The cross is also Christ's exaltation—listen again to his own words: "When I am lifted up, I will draw all men

to myself." You see then that the cross is the glory and
the exaltation of Christ.

✳ ANDREW OF CRETE (CA. 660–740)

12

If There Had Been No Cross

If there had been no cross, Christ would not have been crucified. If there had been no cross, Life would not have been nailed to the tree. If he had not been nailed, the streams of everlasting life would not have welled from his side, blood and water, the cleansing of the world; the record of our sins would not have been canceled, we would not have gained freedom, we would not have enjoyed the tree of life, paradise would not have been opened. If there had been no cross, death would not have been trodden underfoot, the underworld would not have yielded up its spoils.

How great the cross, through which we have received a multitude of blessings, because, against all reckoning, the miracles and sufferings of Christ have been victorious! How precious, the means of God's suffering, and his trophy of victory! On it of his own will he suffered unto death. On it he won his victory, wounding the devil, and conquering death, and shattering the bars of the underworld. The cross has become the common salvation of the whole world.

✳ ANDREW OF CRETE (CA. 660–740)

13

We Stand in Need of His Mercy

The first step in contemplation, dearly beloved, is to consider steadily what God wants, what is pleasing to him, what is acceptable in his sight. And since we all make many mistakes and the boldness of our will revolts against the rightness of his, and since the two cannot be brought into agreement and made to fit together, let us humble ourselves under the mighty hand of the most high God. In the sight of his mercy, let us take pains to show how in all things we stand in need of his mercy, saying: "Heal me, O Lord, and I shall be healed; save me and I shall be saved," and, "O Lord, be gracious to me, heal me, for I have sinned against you."

Once the eye of our heart has been cleansed by dwelling on thoughts of this kind, we are no longer left in bitterness in our own spirit, but we have great joy in the Spirit of God. We do not now consider what is God's will for us, but what God's will is, in itself.

"Life is in his will." Hence we may be sure that what is in harmony with his will is both useful and beneficial for us. It follows that we must take as much care never to deviate from that will as we do to preserve the life of our soul.

✳ BERNARD OF CLAIRVAUX (1090–1153)

14

How the Soul Shows Its Powers according to the Powers of the Body

The soul now shows its powers according to the powers of the body, so that in a person's infancy it produces simplicity, in his youth strength, and in adulthood, when all the person's veins are full, it shows its strongest powers in wisdom; as the tree in its first shoots is tender and then shows that it can bear fruit, and finally, in its full unity, bears it. But then in human old age, when the marrow and veins start to incline in weakness, the soul's powers are gentler, as if from a weariness at human knowledge; as when winter approaches, the sap of the tree diminishes in the branches and leaves, and the tree in its old age begins to bend.

✴ HILDEGARD OF BINGEN (1098–1179)

15

The Creator's Power

You, all-accomplishing
Word of the Father,
are the light of primordial
daybreak over the spheres.
You, the foreknowing
mind of divinity,
foresaw all your works
as you willed them,
your prescience hidden
in the heart of your power,
your power like a wheel around the world,
whose circling never began
and never slides to an end.

✳ HILDEGARD OF BINGEN (1098–1179)

16

To the Trinity Be Praise!

To the Trinity be praise!
  God is music, God is life
  that nurtures every creature in its kind.
Our God is the song of the angel throng
  and the splendor of secret ways
  hid from all humankind,
But God our life is the life of all.

✳ HILDEGARD OF BINGEN (1098–1179)

17

Prayer of St. Francis

Lord, make me an instrument of your peace.

Where there is hatred, let me sow love.

Where there is injury, pardon.

Where there is doubt, faith.

Where there is despair, hope.

Where there is darkness, light.

Where there is sadness, joy.

O Divine Master, grant that I may not so much seek

to be consoled, as to console;

to be understood, as to understand;

to be loved, as to love;

for it is in giving that we receive,

it is in pardoning that we are pardoned,

it is in dying that we are born to eternal life.

✳ ATTRIBUTED TO FRANCIS OF ASSISI (CA. 1181–1226)

18

Canticle of the Sun

Most High, all-powerful, good Lord,

Yours are the praises, the glory, the honor, and all
blessing.

To You alone, Most High, do they belong,

and no man is worthy to mention Your name.

Praised be You, my Lord, with all your creatures,

especially Sir Brother Sun,

Who is the day and through whom You give us light.

And he is beautiful and radiant with great splendor;

and bears a likeness of You, Most High One.

Praised be You, my Lord, through Sister Moon and the
stars,

in heaven You formed them clear and precious and
beautiful.

Praised be You, my Lord, through Brother Wind,
and through the air, cloudy and serene, and every kind
   of weather
through which You give sustenance to Your creatures.
Praised be You, my Lord, through Sister Water,
which is very useful and humble and precious and
   chaste.
Praised be You, my Lord, through Brother Fire,
through whom You light the night
and he is beautiful and playful and robust and strong.
Praised be You, my Lord, through our Sister Mother
   Earth,
who sustains and governs us,
and who produces varied fruits with colored flowers and
   herbs.
Praised be You, my Lord, through those who give
   pardon for Your love
and bear infirmity and tribulation.

Blessed are those who endure in peace

for by You, Most High, they shall be crowned.

Praised be You, my Lord, through our Sister Bodily
    Death,

from whom no living man can escape.

Woe to those who die in mortal sin.

Blessed are those whom death will find in Your most
    holy will,

for the second death shall do them no harm.

Praise and bless my Lord and give Him thanks

and serve Him with great humility.

✳ FRANCIS OF ASSISI (CA. 1181–1226)

19

How Wonderful This Banquet

The only-begotten Son of God, wishing to enable us to share in his divinity, assumed our nature, so that by becoming man he might make men gods.

Moreover, he turned the whole of our nature, which he assumed, to our salvation. For he offered his body to God the Father on the altar of the cross as a sacrifice for our reconciliation; and he shed his blood for our ransom and our cleansing, so that we might be redeemed from wretched captivity and cleansed from all sins.

Now in order that we might always keep the memory of this great act of love, he left his body as food and his blood as drink, to be received by the faithful under the appearances of bread and wine.

How precious and wonderful is this banquet, which brings us salvation and is full of all delight! What could be more precious? It is not the meat of calves or kids that is offered, as happened under the Old Law; at this meal Christ, the true God, is set before us for us to eat. What could be more wonderful than this sacrament?

No sacrament contributes more to our salvation than this; for it purges away our sins, increases our virtues, and nourishes our minds with an abundance of all the spiritual gifts.

✳ THOMAS AQUINAS (CA. 1225–74)

20

Friendship

Friendship is the source of the greatest pleasures, and without friends even the most agreeable pursuits become tedious.

✳ THOMAS AQUINAS (CA. 1225–74)

21

God's Goodness Reflected in His Creatures

Because the divine goodness could not be adequately represented by one creature alone, God produced many and diverse creatures, that what was wanting in one in the representation of the divine goodness might be supplied by another. For goodness, which in God is simple and uniform, in creatures is manifold and divided. Thus the whole universe together participates in the divine goodness more perfectly and represents it better than any single creature whatever.

✳ THOMAS AQUINAS (CA. 1225–74)

22

Inferno

Midway this way of life we're bound upon,
I woke to find myself in a dark wood,
Where the right road was wholly lost and gone.

Ay me! how hard to speak of it—that rude
And rough and stubborn forest! the mere breath
Of memory stirs the old fear in the blood;

It is so bitter, it goes nigh to death;
Yet there I gained such good, that, to convey
The tale, I'll write what else I found therewith.

How I got into it I cannot say,
Because I was so heavy and full of sleep
When first I stumbled from the narrow way;

But when at last I stood beneath a steep
Hill's side, which closed that valley's wandering maze
Whose dread had pierced me to the heart-root deep,

Then I looked up, and saw the morning rays
Mantle its shoulder from that planet bright
Which guides men's feet aright on all their ways.

✳ DANTE ALIGHIERI (1265–1321)

23

Paradiso

O Light Eternal fixed in Self alone,
known only to Yourself, and knowing Self,
You love and glow, knowing and being known!

That circling which, as I conceived it, shone
In You as Your own first reflected light
when I had looked deep into It a while,

seemed in Itself and in Its own Self-color
to be depicted with man's very image.
My eyes were totally absorbed in It.

As the geometer who tries so hard
to square the circle, but cannot discover,
think as he may, the principle involved,

so did I strive with this new mystery:
I yearned to know how could our image fit
into the circle, how could it conform;

but my own wings could not take me so high—
then a great flash of understanding struck
my mind, and suddenly its wish was granted.

At this point power failed high fantasy
but, like a wheel in perfect balance turning,
I felt my will and my desire impelled
by the Love that moves the sun and the other stars.

✳ DANTE ALIGHIERI (1265–1321)

24
A Cloud of Unknowing

B ut now you put me a question and say: "How might I think of him in himself, and what is he?" And to this I can only answer thus: "I have no idea." For with your question you have brought me into that same darkness, into that same cloud of unknowing where I would you were yourself. For a man may, by grace, have the fullness of knowledge of all other creatures and their works, yes, and of the works of God's own self, and he is well able to reflect on them. But no man can think of God himself. Therefore, it is my wish to leave everything that I can think of and choose for my love the thing that I cannot think. Because he can certainly be loved, but not thought. He can be taken and held by love but not by thought. Therefore, though it is good at times to think of the kindness and worthiness of God in particular, and though this is a light and a part of contemplation, nevertheless, in this exercise, it must be cast down and covered over with a cloud of forgetting. You are to step above it stalwartly but lovingly, and with a devout, pleasing, impulsive love strive to pierce that darkness above you. You are to smite upon that thick cloud of unknowing with a sharp dart of longing love. Do not leave that work for anything that may happen.

✴ FROM *THE CLOUD OF UNKNOWING* (FOURTEENTH CENTURY)

25

The Hazelnut

At this time our Lord showed me an inward sight of his homely loving. I saw that he is everything that is good and comforting to us. He is our clothing. In his love he wraps and holds us. He enfolds us in love, and he will never let us go.

And then he showed me a little thing, the size of a hazelnut, in the palm of my hand—and it was as round as a ball. I looked at it with my mind's eye and I thought: "What can this be?" and answer came: "It is all that is made." I marveled that it could last, for I thought it might have crumbled to nothing, it was so small. And the answer came into my mind: "It lasts, and ever shall, because God loves it." And so all things have being through the love of God.

In this little thing I saw three truths. The first is that God made it. The second is that God loves it. And the third is that God looks after it.

✳ JULIAN OF NORWICH (CA. 1342–CA. 1420)

26

The Soul's Three Powers

You drew us out of your holy mind
like a flower
petaled with our soul's three powers,
and into each power
you put the whole plant,
so that they might bear fruit in your garden,
might come back to you
with the fruit you gave them.
And you would come back to the soul
to fill her with your blessedness.
There the soul dwells—
like the fish in the sea
and the sea in the fish.
You gave us memory

so that we might be able to hold your blessings
and so bring forth the flower of glory to your name
and the fruit of profit to ourselves.
You gave us understanding
to understand your truth
and your will—
your will that wants only that we be made holy—
so that we might bear first the flower of glory
and then the fruit of virtue.
And you gave us our will
so that we might be able to love
what our understanding has seen
and what our memory has held.

✳ CATHERINE OF SIENA (CA. 1347–80)

27

Look for Jesus, Not Yourself

In life and in death keep close to Jesus and give yourself into his faithful keeping; he alone can help you when all others fail you. He is of such a kind, this beloved friend of yours, that he will not share your love with another; he wishes to have your heart for himself alone, to reign there like a king seated on his rightful throne. If only you knew the way to empty your heart of all things created! If you did, how gladly would Jesus come and make his home with you!

When you put your trust in men, excluding Jesus, you will find that it is nearly all a complete loss. Have no faith in a reed that shakes in the wind, don't try leaning upon it; mortal things are but grass, remember, the glory of them is but grass in flower and will fall. Look only at a man's outward guise and you will quickly be led astray; look to others to console you and bring you benefit, and as often as not you will find you have suffered loss.

If you look for Jesus in everything, you will certainly find him; but if it's yourself you're looking for, it's yourself you're going to find, and that to your own hurt, because a man is a greater bane to himself, if he doesn't look for Jesus, than the whole world is, or the whole host of his enemies.

✻ THOMAS À KEMPIS (CA. 1380–1471)

28

Make Room for Christ

Come then, faithful soul, prepare your heart for this your Spouse, so that he may vouchsafe to come to you and dwell within you.

For so he says: "If any man love me, he will keep my word; and we will come to him and make our dwelling ith him."

Make room therefore for Christ, and refuse entrance to all others.

When you have Christ, you are rich and have need of nought else.

He will provide for you, and be in all things your faithful procurator; you shall not need to look to men.

Put your whole trust in God; let him be your fear and your love.

✳ THOMAS À KEMPIS (CA. 1380–1471)

29
The Gift of Christ's Body

Suppose that this most holy Sacrament were celebrated in one place only; suppose there were only one priest in the whole world to say the words of consecration. How men would long to go to that place, to visit that one priest of God and see the divine mysteries celebrated! But now there are many priests, and in many places Christ is offered, so that the farther afield Holy Communion is spread throughout the world, the greater proof it may yield of God's grace and love for men. Thank you, O good Jesus, eternal shepherd, for deigning to refresh us poor outcasts with your precious body and blood; for inviting us with your own lips to partake of this mystery, when you say: Come to me, all you that labor and are burdened; I will give you rest. . . .

O Jesus, sweetest, kindest, what great worship and thanksgiving we ought to show you, what never-ending praise, in return for the gift of your holy body! There is not a man to be found able to unfold in words its wonderful power.

✳ THOMAS À KEMPIS (CA. 1380–1471)

30

Not Counting the Cost

Teach us, good Lord, to serve Thee
as Thou deservest,
to give and not to count the cost;
to fight and not to heed the wounds;
to toil and not to seek for rest;
to labor and not to ask for any reward
save that of knowing that we do Thy will.

✳ IGNATIUS OF LOYOLA (1491–1556)

31

Thy Love and Thy Grace

Take, Lord, and receive all my liberty,

my memory, my understanding, and my entire will,

all that I have and possess.

Thou hast given all to me.

To Thee, O Lord, I return it.

All is Thine, dispose of it wholly according to Thy will.

Give me Thy love and Thy grace,

for this is sufficient for me.

✳ IGNATIUS OF LOYOLA (1491–1556)

32

Love into Practice

Love consists in sharing
what one has
and what one is
with those one loves.

Love ought to show itself in deeds
more than in words.

✴ IGNATIUS OF LOYOLA (1491–1556)

33
The Five Points

We must continually examine our affections, thoughts, words, and deeds, so as to come to an accurate knowledge of our old and of our new man. But I urge on you as a kind of commandment that you make this examination every night before going to bed. You must demand of yourself a strict account of the day. In the presence of your Judge who will one day appear, you must reprove, accuse, and convict yourself of what you have done wrong. And give thanks to God through Jesus Christ for what you have done or thought well.

You should faithfully perform the examination and spend fifteen minutes on it. Its form comprises these five points:

1. You should thank God for the benefits you have received that day, recalling and going over them one by one.

2. You should ask God for grace to recognize and feel your sins committed that day.

3. You should turn to your own heart and demand a detailed accounting of your soul for your thoughts, words, and actions, noting those which seem deserving of reproof before God and his representative.

4. You should ask God's mercy on these sins of commission and omission.

5. You should resolve upon some good emendation of these sins and also upon mentioning in confession those that require the confessor's jurisdiction and judgment, such as all certain or doubtful mortal sins. At the end, say an Our Father and a Hail Mary for the remission of your sins.

✳ PETER FAVRE (1506–46)

34
Be Cordial to Others

So far as you can without offending God, try to be genial and to behave in such a way with those you have to deal with that they may take pleasure in your conversation and may wish to imitate your life and manners, instead of being frightened and deterred from virtue.

The more holy someone is, the more cordial should they be with others.

Although you may be pained because their conversation is not what you would wish, never keep aloof if you want to help them and win their love.

Try to think rightly about God. . . . He does not look at such trifling matters as you suppose; do not alarm your soul or lose courage, for you might lose greatly. Keep a pure intention and a firm resolve not to offend God, as I said, but do not trammel your soul, for instead of advancing in sanctity you would contract a number of imperfections and would not help others as you might have done.

※ TERESA OF ÁVILA (1515–82)

35
Win Others by Example

It is plainly wrong to meet non-Catholics with bitterness or to treat them with discourtesy. For this is nothing else than the reverse of Christ's example because it breaks the bruised reed and quenches the smoking flax. We ought to instruct with meekness those whom heresy has made bitter and suspicious and has estranged from orthodox Catholics, especially from our fellow Jesuits. Thus, by wholehearted charity and good will we may win them over to us in the Lord.

Again, it is a mistaken policy to behave in a contentious fashion and to start disputes about matters of belief with argumentative people who are disposed by their very natures to wrangling. Indeed, the fact of their being so constituted is a reason the more why such people should be attracted and won to the simplicity of the faith as much by example as by argument.

✳ PETER CANISIUS (1521–97)

36

Rush to the Father's Arms

REFLECTION ON PSALM 91:

"HE WHO DWELLS IN THE SHELTER OF THE MOST HIGH"

Notice that what is said is not "he who trusts" . . . but "he who dwells." This is to convince us that we are not to fly to the divine protection as men do to a tree or a doorway when it rains, but rather as little boys who rush to their father's arms when anything frightens them. They know that they have mother and father there who would gladly give their hearts' blood to protect them.

But people who seek refuge from rain under a tree, have a good look round first. It is only when no better shelter is available that they run willy-nilly to the tree. Why is it that some men implore divine assistance without receiving it, and seem to put their trust in God without being protected by him? The reason is that they do not really dwell in the aid of the Most High, nor take shelter under the providence of God as in their Father's house. They rather make sporadic dashes to it in time of trouble, as they do to a tree when there is a sudden shower. It is therefore very necessary for us to get into the way of always and instinctively turning to God.

✴ ROBERT BELLARMINE (1542–1621)

37
When Prayer Is Dry

There are three tests to ascertain whether dryness in prayer is the result of God's purgation or of our own sins.

The first is when we find no comfort either in the things of God or in created things. For when God brings the soul into the dark night in order to wean it from sweetness and to purify its sensual desires, he does not allow it to find sweetness or comfort anywhere.

The second is that the memory is ordinarily centered on God with painful anxiety and carefulness. The spirit becomes strong, more vigilant, and more careful lest there be any negligence in serving God.

The third sign is inability to meditate or make reflections, and to excite the imagination as before, despite all the efforts we may make. For God now begins to communicate himself, no longer through the channels of sense as formerly, but in pure spirit.

✳ JOHN OF THE CROSS (1542–91)

38
Apply Your Mind to God Alone

The more God gives, the more he makes us desire, until we are empty and he is able to fill us with good things.

The immense benefits of God can only be contained by empty and solitary hearts. Therefore our Lord, who loves you greatly, wishes you to be quite alone, for he desires to be your only companion.

You must needs apply your mind to him alone, and in him alone content yourself, that in him you may find all consolation. Although God is always with us, if we set our hearts on other things beside him we cannot be at peace.

God knows what is best for all and orders affairs for our good. Think on this only, that all is ordained by God.

And pour in love where there is no love, and you will draw love out.

✳ JOHN OF THE CROSS (1542–91)

39
True Longevity

True longevity is reckoned not by number of years but according to progress in virtue. If the Lord of Heaven grants me one day more of life, He does so that I may correct yesterday's faults; failure to do this would be a sign of great ingratitude.

✳ MATTEO RICCI (1552–1610)

40

On the Eucharist

I have not yet said anything about the most sacred of all devotions—the holy and sacred sacrifice and sacrament of the Eucharist, the heart of the Christian religion. It is an ineffable mystery that embraces the untold depths of divine love, and in which God, giving himself to us, bestows freely upon us all his blessings and graces.

Prayer united to this divine sacrifice has unutterable power. Endeavor if possible to be present each day at holy Mass, so that together with the priest you may offer the sacrifice of your Redeemer to God his Father on your own behalf and that of the whole Church. What a privilege it is to be united in so blessed and mighty an action!

✳ FRANCIS DE SALES (1567–1622)

41
Guardian Angels

There is no creature, no matter how mean, vile, or abject, faithful or unfaithful, who has not his angel to guard him and to urge him continually to do right.

These blessed spirits offer our prayers to the divine Goodness; they kindle in our hearts the love of virtue; they strengthen us and obtain for us the courage and vigor to practice it—if we are sad and in adversity, they are ever near, to cheer us and exhort us to patience. They never cease to inspire us with good thoughts, to help us to make progress in divine love; until at last we reach the heavenly country, to dwell forever in their company.

This is what they desire, knowing that for this end we were created. They are so jealous of our happiness that they rejoice when they see that we are faithful to

God and that we are corresponding with his love; and when we do not, if they could grieve they would. It is to our guardian angels that we owe all our good inspirations, suitable to our vocation and circumstances.

✳ FRANCIS DE SALES (1567–1622)

42

The Simplicity of a Dove

Jesus, the Lord, expects us to have the simplicity of a dove. This means giving a straightforward opinion about things in the way we honestly see them, without needless reservations. It also means doing things without double-dealing or manipulation, our intention being focused solely on God. Each of us, then, should take care to behave always in the spirit of simplicity, remembering that God likes to deal with the simple, and that he conceals the secrets of heaven from the wise and prudent of this world and reveals them to little ones.

But while Christ recommends a dove's simplicity, he also tells us to have a serpent's prudence. He means that we should speak and behave with discretion. We ought, therefore, to keep quiet about matters which should not be made known, especially if they are unsuitable or unlawful. When we are discussing things which it is good and proper to talk about we should hold back any details which would not be for God's glory, or which could harm some other person, or which would make us foolishly smug.

In actual practice this virtue is about choosing the right way to do things. We should make it a sacred principle, then, admitting no exceptions, that since we are working for God we will always choose God-related ways for carrying out our work, and see and judge things from Christ's point of view and not from a worldly-wise one; and not according to the feeble reasoning of our own mind.

✳ VINCENT DE PAUL (CA. 1580–1660)

43

God Will Love Us on Account of the Poor

We should not judge the poor by their clothes and their outward appearance nor by their mental capacity, since they are often ignorant and uncouth. On the contrary, if you consider the poor in the light of faith, then you will see that they take the place of God the Son, who chose to be poor. Indeed, in his passion, having lost even the appearance of man, foolishness to the Gentiles and a scandal to the Jews, he showed he was to preach the gospel to the poor in these words: "He has sent me to preach good news to the poor." Therefore we should be of the same mind and should imitate what Christ did, caring for the poor, consoling them, helping them, and guiding them.

Christ chose to be born in poverty and took poor men as his disciples; he himself became the servant of the poor and so shared their condition that whatever good or harm was done to the poor, he said he would consider done to himself. Since God loves the poor, he also loves the lovers of the poor: when someone loves another, he loves too those who love or serve that other. So we too hope that God will love us on account of the poor. We visit them then; we strive to concern ourselves with the weak and the needy; we so share their sufferings that with the apostle we feel we have become all things to all men. Therefore we must strive to be deeply involved in the cares and sorrows of our neighbor and pray to God to inspire us with compassion and pity, filling our hearts and keeping them full.

✳ VINCENT DE PAUL (CA. 1580–1660)

44

Grace Follows after Sorrow

The Lord, our Savior, raised his voice and spoke with incomparable majesty. "Let all know," he said, "that after sorrow grace follows; let them understand that without the burden of affliction one cannot arrive at the height of glory; that the measure of heavenly gifts is increased in proportion to the labors undertaken. Let them be on their guard against error or deception; this is the only ladder by which paradise is reached; without the cross there is no road to heaven."

✳ ROSE OF LIMA (1586–1617)

45
The Little Things

We must not grow weary of doing the little things for the love of God, who looks not on the great size of the work, but on the love in it.

✳ BROTHER LAWRENCE (1614–91)

46

Peace of Heart That Surpasses Every Treasure

Do you find that you are making no progress in prayer? Let it be enough for you to offer to God the prayer that our Savior makes for us in the most holy sacrament of the altar, using his fervent offering to make reparation for your own lukewarmness. And whenever you do anything, pray in this way: "My God, I am going to do this or endure that in the sacred heart of your divine Son and according to his holy intentions, which I offer you to make reparation for whatever evil or imperfection there may be in my own deeds." Continue in this way in all the circumstances of life. And whenever anything happens to you that is painful, hard to bear, or mortifying, tell yourself this: "Accept what the Sacred

Heart of Jesus sends you in order to unite you to himself."

But above all things maintain peace of heart that surpasses every treasure. For maintaining this peace, nothing is more effective than to renounce one's own will and to set in its place the will of the Sacred Heart, so that he may do for us whatever redounds to his glory and that we may joyfully submit to him and place in him our full confidence.

✳ MARGARET MARY ALACOQUE (1647–90)

47

Give Yourself to the Present

To escape the distress caused by regret for the past or fear about the future, this is the rule to follow: leave the past to the infinite mercy of God, the future to his good providence; give the present wholly to his love by being faithful to his grace.

When God in his goodness sends you some disappointment, one of those trials that used to annoy you so much, before everything thank him for it as for a great favor all the more useful for the great work of your perfection in that it completely overturns the work of the moment.

✻ JEAN-PIERRE DE CAUSSADE (1675–1751)

48

Lead, Kindly Light

Lead, kindly Light, amid the encircling gloom,
Lead thou me on;
The night is dark, and I am far from home,
Lead thou me on.
Keep thou my feet; I do not ask to see
The distant scene; one step enough for me.

I was not ever thus, nor prayed that thou
Shouldst lead me on;
I loved to choose and see my path; but now
Lead thou me on.
I loved the garish day, and, spite of fears,
Pride ruled my will: remember not past years.
So long thy power hath blest me, sure it still

Will lead me on
O'er moor and fen, o'er crag and torrent, till
The night is gone,
And with the morn those Angel faces smile,
Which I have loved long since, and lost awhile.

✴ JOHN HENRY NEWMAN (1801–90)

49

God Has Created Me to Do Him Some Definite Service

God has created me to do Him some definite service;

He has committed some work to me which He has not
committed to another.

I have my mission—I may never know it in this life,

but I shall be told it in the next.

I am a link in a chain, a bond of connection between
persons.

He has not created me for nothing. I shall do good. I
shall do His work.

I shall be an angel of peace, a preacher of truth in my
own place,

if I do but keep His commandments.

Therefore, I will trust Him.

Whatever, wherever I am. I can never be thrown away.

If I am in sickness, my sickness may serve Him.

In perplexity, my perplexity may serve Him;

if I am in sorrow, my sorrow may serve Him.

He does nothing in vain. He knows what He is about.

He may take away my friends, throw me among
strangers.

He may make me feel desolate, make my spirits sink,
hide my future from me,

still He knows what He is about.

❋ JOHN HENRY NEWMAN (1801–90)

50
Learning from the Poor

There is a useful method for strengthening hearts that lack courage. This is to give them the privilege of seeing the poor, of being shown Our Lord Jesus Christ not only in holy pictures painted by great artists but of being shown Jesus Christ and his wounds in the person of the poor.

The sons of noblemen must learn what it means to be hungry and thirsty or to live in an attic without clothing or furniture. They must be able to see dire poverty in the guise of sick children, of children who are weeping. They must be able to see them and to love them.

✳ Antoine Frédéric Ozanam (1813–53)

51

As Kingfishers Catch Fire

As kingfishers catch fire, dragonflies draw flame;
   As tumbled over rim in roundy wells
   Stones ring; like each tucked string tells, each hung
      bell's
Bow swung finds tongue to fling out broad its name;
Each mortal thing does one thing and the same;
   Deals out that being indoors each one dwells;
   Selves—goes itself; *myself* it speaks and spells;
Crying *What I do is me: for that I came.*

I say more: the just man justices;
   Keeps grace: that keeps all his goings graces;
Acts in God's eye what in God's eye he is—

Christ—for Christ plays in ten thousand places,
Lovely in limbs, and lovely in eyes not his
   To the Father through the features of men's faces.

✳ GERARD MANLEY HOPKINS (1844–89)

52
God's Glory in Work

When a man is in God's grace and free from mortal sin, then everything that he does, as long as there is no sin in it, gives God glory. . . . It is not only prayer that gives God glory but work. Smiting on an anvil, sawing a beam, whitewashing a wall, driving horses, sweeping, scouring, everything gives God some glory if being in his grace you do it as your duty. . . . To lift up the hands in prayer gives God glory, but a man with a dung fork in his hand, a woman with a slop pail, gives him glory too. He is so great that all things give him glory if you mean they should.

✳ GERARD MANLEY HOPKINS (1844–89)

53
God's Grandeur

The world is charged with the grandeur of God.
  It will flame out, like shining from shook foil;
  It gathers to a greatness, like the ooze of oil
Crushed. Why do men then now not reck his rod?
Generations have trod, have trod, have trod;
  And all is seared with trade; bleared, smeared with
    toil;
  And wears man's smudge and shares man's smell: the
    soil
Is bare now, nor can foot feel, being shod.

And for all this, nature is never spent;
  There lives the dearest freshness deep down things;
And though the last lights off the black West went

Oh, morning, at the brown brink eastward, springs—
Because the Holy Ghost over the bent
  World broods with warm breast and with ah! bright
    wings.

✳ GERARD MANLEY HOPKINS (1844–89)

54
Pied Beauty

Glory be to God for dappled things—
   For skies of couple-color as a brinded cow;
      For rose-moles all in stipple upon trout that swim;
Fresh-firecoal chestnut-falls; finches' wings;
   Landscape plotted and pieced—fold, fallow, and plough;
      And all trades, their gear and tackle and trim.

All things counter, original, spare, strange;
   Whatever is fickle, freckled (who knows how?)
      With swift, slow; sweet, sour; adazzle, dim;
He fathers-forth whose beauty is past change:
            Praise him.

✶ GERARD MANLEY HOPKINS (1844–89)

55

Prayer of Abandonment

Father,

I abandon myself into your hands,

do with me what you will.

Whatever you may do, I thank you:

I am ready for all, I accept all.

Let only your will be done in me

and in all your creatures.

I wish no more than this, O Lord.

Into your hands, I commend my soul;

I offer it to you

with all the love of my heart;

for I love you, Lord,

and so need to give myself:

to surrender myself into your hands

without reserve and with boundless confidence: for you are my father.

✻ CHARLES DE FOUCAULD (1858–1916)

56

Pray as You Can

Prayer, in the sense of union with God, is the most crucifying thing there is. One must do it for God's sake; but one will not get any satisfaction out of it, in the sense of feeling "I am good at prayer," "I have an infallible method." That would be disastrous, since what we want to learn is precisely our own weakness, powerlessness, unworthiness. Nor ought one to expect "a sense of the reality of the supernatural" of which you speak. And one should wish for no prayer, except precisely the prayer that God gives us—probably very distracted and unsatisfactory in every way!

On the other hand, the only way to pray is to pray; and the way to pray well is to pray much. If one has no time for this, then one must at least pray regularly.

But the less one prays, the worse it goes. And if circumstances do not permit even regularity, then one must put up with the fact that when one does try to pray, one can't pray—and our prayer will probably consist of telling this to God.

The rule is simply: *Pray as you can, and do not try to pray as you can't.*

Take yourself as you find yourself, and start from that.

✳ JOHN CHAPMAN (1865–1933)

57
How to Pray

The power of prayer is indeed wonderful. It is like a queen, who, having free access always to the king, can obtain whatever she asks. To secure a hearing there is no need to recite set prayers composed for the occasion—were this the case, I should indeed deserve to be pitied!

Apart from the Office [the daily prayer of the church], which is a daily joy, I do not have the courage to search through books for beautiful prayers. They are so numerous that it would only make my head ache. Unable either to say them all or to choose between them, I do as a child would who cannot read—I just say what I want to say to God, quite simply, and he never fails to understand.

For me, prayer is an uplifting of the heart, a glance toward heaven, a cry of gratitude and love in times of sorrow as well as joy. It is something noble, something supernatural, which expands the soul and unites it to God.

When my state of spiritual aridity is such that not a single good thought will come, I repeat very slowly the Our Father and the Hail Mary, which are enough to console me and provide food for my soul.

✳ THÉRÈSE OF LISIEUX (1873–97)

58

Be Not Afraid to Tell Jesus

Be not afraid to tell Jesus that you love Him; even though it be without feeling, this is the way to oblige Him to help you, and carry you like a little child too feeble to walk.

✳ THÉRÈSE OF LISIEUX (1873–97)

59

Love the One You Dislike

In the Gospel the Lord showed me clearly what his new commandment demands. I read in St. Matthew: "You have heard it said that you should love your neighbor and hate your enemy; but I say to you, love your enemies and pray for those who persecute you."

We all have our natural likes and dislikes. We may feel more drawn to one person and may be tempted to go a long way around to avoid meeting another. Well, the Lord tells me that the latter is the one I must love and pray for, even though the manner shown me leads me to believe that the person does not care for me. "If you love those that love you, what thanks are due to you? For sinners also love those who love them" (Luke 6:32).

Nor is it enough to love. We must prove our love. We take a natural delight in pleasing friends, but that is not love; even sinners do the same.

✳ THÉRÈSE OF LISIEUX (1873–97)

60

My Vocation Is Love

All the gifts of heaven, even the most perfect of them, without love, are absolutely nothing; charity is the best way of all, because it leads straight to God. . . . When St. Paul was talking about the different members of the mystical body I couldn't recognize myself in any of them; or rather I could recognize myself in all of them. But charity—that was the key to my vocation. If the Church was a body composed of different members, it couldn't lack the noblest of all; it must have a heart, and a heart burning with love. And I realized that this love was the true motive force that enabled the other members of the Church to act; if it ceased to function the apostles would forget to preach the gospel, the martyrs would refuse to shed their blood.

Love, in fact, is the vocation that includes all others; it's a universe of its own, comprising all time and space—it's eternal. Beside myself with joy, I cried out: "Jesus, my love! I've found my vocation, and my vocation is love." I had discovered where it is that I belong in the Church, the niche God has appointed for me. To be nothing else than love, deep down in the heart of Mother Church; that's to be everything at once—my dream wasn't a dream after all.

✳ Thérèse of Lisieux (1873–97)

61

A Dazzling Darkness

Lord Jesus, when it was given me to see where the dazzling trail of particular beauties and partial harmonies was leading, I recognized that it was all coming to center on a single point, a single person: yourself. Every presence makes me feel that you are near me; every touch is the touch of your hand; every necessity transmits to me a pulsation of your will.

That the Spirit may always shine forth in me, that I may not succumb to the temptation that lies in wait for every act of boldness, nor ever forget that you alone must be sought in and through everything, you, Lord, will send me—at what moments only you know—deprivations, disappointments, sorrow.

What is to be brought about is more than a simple union: it is a transformation, in the course of which the only thing our human activity can do is, humbly, to make ourselves ready, and to accept.

✳ PIERRE TEILHARD DE CHARDIN (1881–1955)

62

God in the Tip of My Pen

God, in all that is most living and incarnate in him, is not far away from us, altogether apart from the world we see, touch, hear, smell, and taste around us. Rather he awaits us in every instant in our action, in the work of the moment. There is a sense in which he is at the tip of my pen, my spade, my brush, my needle. By pressing the stroke, the line, or the stitch on which I am engaged to its ultimate natural finish, I shall lay hold of that last end toward which my innermost will tends.

✴ Pierre Teilhard de Chardin (1881–1955)

63
Losing Hold

[W]hen I feel I am losing hold of myself
and am absolutely passive within the hands
of the great unknown forces that have formed me;
in all those dark moments, O God,
grant that I may understand that it is you
(provided only my faith is strong enough)
who are painfully parting the fibers of my being
in order to penetrate to the very marrow
of my substance and bear me away within yourself.

✳ PIERRE TEILHARD DE CHARDIN (1881–1955)

64
That I May See

Lord grant that I may see, that I may see you, that I may see and experience you present and animating all things. . . . Jesus, help me to perfect the perception and expression of my vision. . . . Help me to the right action, the right word, help me to give the example that will reveal you best.

✳ PIERRE TEILHARD DE CHARDIN (1881–1955)

65

Trust in the Slow Work of God

Above all, trust in the slow work of God.

We are quite naturally impatient in everything

    to reach the end without delay.

We should like to skip the intermediate stages.

We are impatient of being on the way to something

    unknown, something new.

And yet it is the law of all progress

    that it is made by passing through

    some stages of instability—

    and that it may take a very long time.

And so I think it is with you.

Your ideas mature gradually—let them grow,

    let them shape themselves, without undue haste.

Don't try to force them on,
    as though you could be today what time
    (that is to say, grace and circumstances
    acting on your own good will)
    will make of you tomorrow.

Only God could say what this new spirit
    gradually forming within you will be.
Give Our Lord the benefit of believing
    that his hand is leading you,
and accept the anxiety of feeling yourself
    in suspense and incomplete.

✳ PIERRE TEILHARD DE CHARDIN (1881–1955)

66

Pilgrim Soul

No pilgrim soul can worthily love God. But when a soul does everything possible and trusts in divine mercy, why would Jesus reject such a spirit? Has he not commanded us to love God according to our strength? If you have given and consecrated everything to God, why be afraid?

✳ PADRE PIO (1887–1968)

67

Do Not Listen to These Temptations

When the soul grieves and is afraid of offending God, it does not offend Him and is very far from committing sin. Divine grace is with you continually and you are very dear to the Lord. Shadows and fears and convictions to the contrary are diabolical stratagems that you should despise in the name of Jesus. Do not listen to these temptations. The spirit of evil is busily engaged in trying to make you believe that your past life has been all strewn with sins. . . .

Never fall back on yourself alone, but place all your trust in God and don't be too eager to be set free from your present state. Let the Holy Spirit act within you. Give yourself up to all his transports and have no fear. He is so wise and gentle and discreet that He never brings about anything but good. How good this Holy Spirit, this Comforter, is to all, but how supremely good He is to those who seek Him!

✳ PADRE PIO (1887–1968)

68

The Ways God Is Present

By the supernatural virtue of Charity, Divine Love dwells in the soul and in a very personal, intimate relationship, for there are several different ways in which God can be present. First of all, God is present everywhere in the world, because He is the Power that made the world, the Wisdom that planned it, and the Love that executed it. God is also present—but personally—in the Eucharist, and in our souls so long as the Sacramental presence lasts. But there is still another Divine presence that is more abiding, and that is the presence of God in the soul through Charity. To be in the state of Grace through Charity does not mean that we have something, but that we are something. For one of the consequences of the Faith is that an extraordinary event happens to us: we receive a Gift. Many baptized souls are ignorant of this mystery and remain ignorant of it throughout their lives; for just as it is possible for some families to live under the same roof and never communicate, so it is also possible for a man to have God in his soul and yet hold little intimate exchange with Him. The more holy souls become, and the more detached from the world, the greater their consciousness of God's presence.

✳ FULTON SHEEN (1895–1979)

69

Love When We Do Not Find Love

Love never gets out of date. Love, therefore, all things, and all persons in God.

So long as there are poor, I am poor;
So long as there are prisons, I am a prisoner;
So long as there are sick, I am weak;
So long as there is ignorance, I must learn the truth;
So long as there is hate, I must love;
So long as there is hunger, I am famished.

Such is the identification Our Divine Lord would have us make with all whom He made in love and for love. Where we do not find love, we must put it. Then everyone is lovable. There is nothing in all the world more calculated to inspire love for others than this Vision of Christ in our fellow man: "For I was hungry, and you gave me to eat; I was thirsty, and you gave me to drink; I was a stranger, and you took me in: Naked, and you covered me: sick and you visited me: I was in prison, and you came to me."

✳ FULTON SHEEN (1895–1979)

70

My First Impulse toward Catholicism

Mrs. Barrett gave me my first impulse toward Catholicism. It was around ten o'clock in the morning that I went up to Kathryn's to call for her to come out and play. There was no one on the porch or in the kitchen. The breakfast dishes had all been washed. They were long railroad apartments, those flats, and thinking the children must be in the front room, I burst in and ran through the bedrooms.

In the front room Mrs. Barrett was on her knees, saying her prayers. She turned to tell me that Kathryn and the children had all gone to the store and went on with her praying. And I felt a warm burst of love toward Mrs. Barrett that I have never forgotten, a feeling of gratitude and happiness that still warms my heart when I remember her. She had God, and there was beauty and joy in her life.

All through my life what she was doing remained with me. And though I became oppressed with the problem of poverty and injustice, though I groaned at the hideous sordidness of man's lot, though there were years when I clung to the philosophy of economic determination as an explanation of man's fate, still there were moments when in the midst of misery and class strife, life was shot through with glory. Mrs. Barrett in her sordid little tenement flat finished her breakfast dishes at ten o'clock in the morning and got down on her knees and prayed to God.

✳ DOROTHY DAY (1897–1980)

71
The Long Loneliness

We cannot love God unless we love each other, and to love we must know each other. We know him in the breaking of bread, and we know each other in the breaking of bread, and we are not alone anymore. Heaven is a banquet and life is a banquet, too, even with a crust, where there is companionship.

We have all known the long loneliness and we have learned that the only solution is love and that love comes with community.

✳ DOROTHY DAY (1897–1980)

72

It's Hard to Love in a Two-Room Apartment

We are not expecting utopia here on this earth. But God meant things to be much easier than we have made them. A man has a natural right to food, clothing, and shelter. A certain amount of goods is necessary to lead a good life. A family needs work as well as bread. Property is proper to man. We must keep repeating these things. Eternal life begins now. "All the way to heaven is heaven, because He said, 'I am the Way.'" The Cross is there of course, but "in the Cross is joy of spirit." And love makes all things easy. If we are putting off the old man and putting on Christ, then we are walking in love, and love is all that we want. But it is hard to love, from the human standpoint and from the divine standpoint, in a two-room apartment.

✳ Dorothy Day (1897–1980)

73
Why We Stand before the Cross

Many pass by the unveiled cross. Many remain. Because they belong there. Because here they have found everything. They stay. They kneel down. . . . Sinners kiss the wounds that they themselves have caused. The murderers flee from their guilt to the murdered One, the executioners to their own victim. And so I go to him. And sinners, who themselves are crucified with him on the cross of their own guilt, speak: "Lord, think of me when you come into your kingdom."

The dying lie at his feet. For they suffer his destiny. They die because he died. True, everyone must die because of sin. But God has allowed this deadly guilt in his kingdom of this world for a reason. He held this world embraced in his love for his incarnate Son, in whose death he was so able to overcome sin through greater grace that the world could not escape his mercy. And therefore death, which we ourselves caused and which we suffer as the wages of sin, is first, last, and always only the death that causes the death of sin.

Those who suffer weep before his cross. What night of need was not his night? What fears are not sanctified by his? To be raised up in hope, what grief needs to know more than that it has been borne by the Son of Man, who is the Son of God?

✳ KARL RAHNER (1904–84)

74
I Have Experienced God

I have encountered God directly and, as well as I could, I wanted to communicate such experiences to others. . . . I have experienced God, the nameless and unfathomable One, silent and yet near to me in Triune self-giving. . . . I have experienced not human words about God, but God's very self. . . . This experience is indeed grace, and there is really no one to whom it is denied. Of this I was quite sure.

✳ KARL RAHNER (1904–84)

75
Love Is a Kind of Dying

The mystery of Christ is the ultimate truth, the reality toward which all human life aspires. And this mystery is known by love. Love is going out of oneself, surrendering the self, letting the reality, the truth, take over. . . . It is not something we achieve for ourselves. It is something that comes when we let go. We have to abandon everything—all words, thoughts, hopes, fears, all attachment to ourselves or to any earthly things, and let the divine mystery take possession of our lives. It feels like death, and it is, in fact, a sort of dying. It is encountering the darkness, the abyss, the void. It is facing absolute nothingness—or as Augustine Baker, the English Benedictine, said, it is "the union of the nothing with the Nothing." This is the negative aspect of contemplation. The positive aspect is, of course, the opposite. It is total fulfillment, total wisdom, total bliss, the answer to all problems, the peace that passes understanding, the joy that is the fullness of love.

✳ BEDE GRIFFITHS (1906–93)

76
The Hand of God

For me Jesus Christ is *everything*. . . . He was and he is my ideal from the moment of my entrance into the Society [of Jesus]. He was and he continues to be my way; he was and he still is my strength. I don't think it is necessary to explain very much what that means. Take Jesus Christ from my life and everything would collapse—like a human body from which someone removed the skeleton, heart, and head. . . .

In Lourdes, I acquired an awareness of the power of God as he intervenes in history.

In Marneffe, after our expulsion from Spain, I lived in a community of 350 persons who wondered each evening if they would have enough food for the following day. And each day, we had enough.

In the Yamaguchi prison, I was alone for thirty-five days, wondering why I was there, for how long, and if, in the end, I might be executed. When this "experience" was over, you could not help but believe in a special Providence.

And immediately after the explosion of the atomic bomb in Hiroshima—shouldn't I remember how we were able to feed and care for so many wounded?

When, in the following years, I traveled throughout the world seeking men and collecting funds for Japan, I was the witness to a rare generosity and to extraordinary sacrifices. One might give many reasons for this, but as for me, I saw in it the hand of God.

✳ PEDRO ARRUPE (1907–91)

77
More than Ever

More than ever I find myself in the hands of God.
This is what I have wanted all my life from my youth.

But now there is a difference;
the initiative is entirely with God.

It is indeed a profound spiritual experience
to know and feel myself so totally in God's hands.

✴ PEDRO ARRUPE (1907–91)
[This prayer was written after he suffered a stroke.]

78

Love Will Decide Everything

Nothing is more practical than finding God, that is than falling in love in a quite absolute, final way. What you are in love with, what seizes your imagination, will affect everything. It will decide what will get you out of bed in the morning, what you do with your evenings, how you spend your weekends, what you read, who you know, what breaks your heart, and what amazes you with joy and gratitude. Fall in love, stay in love, and it will decide everything.

✳ PEDRO ARRUPE (1907–91)

79
The Secret of True Happiness

Do you want to know the secret of true happiness? Of deep and genuine peace? Do you want to solve at a blow all your difficulties in relations with your neighbor, bring all polemic to an end, avoid all dissension?

Well, decide here and now to love things and people as Jesus loved them, that is, to the point of self-sacrifice. Do not bother with the bookkeeping of love; love without keeping accounts.

If you know someone who is decent and likable, love him, but if someone else is very unlikable, love him just the same. If someone greets you and smiles, greet him and smile back, but if someone else treads on your feet, smile just the same. If someone does you a good turn, thank the Lord for it, but if someone else slanders you, persecutes you, curses you, strikes you, thank him and carry on.

Do not say: "I'm right, he's wrong." Say: "I must love him as myself." This is the kind of love Jesus taught: a love that transforms, vivifies, enriches, brings peace.

✳ CARLO CARRETTO (1910–88)

80

Keep Your Lamp Burning

What we need is to love without getting tired. How does a lamp burn? Through the continuous input of small drops of oil. What are these drops of oil in our lamps? They are the small things of daily life: faithfulness, small words of kindness, a thought for others, our way of being silent, of looking, of speaking, and of acting. Do not look for Jesus away from yourselves. He is not out there; He is in you. Keep your lamp burning, and you will recognize Him.

✳ MOTHER TERESA (1910–97)

81
Love Each Other

Love each other as God loves each one of you, with an intense and particular love. Be kind to each other: It is better to commit faults with gentleness than to work miracles with unkindness.

✳ MOTHER TERESA (1910–97)

82
Something Beautiful for God

I f we really want to conquer the world, we will not be able to do it with bombs or with weapons of mass destruction. Let us conquer the world with our love. Let us interweave our lives with bonds of sacrifice and love, and it will be possible for us to conquer the world.

We do not need to carry out grand things in order to show great love for God and for our neighbor. It is the intensity of love we put into our gestures that makes them something beautiful for God.

✴ MOTHER TERESA (1910–97)

83

The Current Is God

Each one of us is merely a small instrument. When you look at the inner workings of electrical things, often you see small and big wires, new and old, cheap and expensive lined up. Until the current passes through them there will be no light. That wire is you and me. The current is God.

We have the power to let the current pass through us, use us, produce light in the world. Or we can refuse to be used and allow darkness to spread.

✳ MOTHER TERESA (1910–97)

84

Letter to Jesus

Dear Jesus,

I have been criticized. "He's a bishop, he's a cardinal," people have said, "he's been writing letters to all kinds of people: to Mark Twain, to Péguy, and heaven knows how many others. And not a line to Jesus Christ!"

Here is my letter. I write it trembling, feeling like a poor deaf mute trying to make himself understood. . . .

When you said: "Blessed are the poor, blessed are the persecuted," I wasn't with you. If I had been, I'd have whispered into your ear: "For heaven's sake, Lord, change the subject, if you want to keep any followers at all. Don't you know that everyone wants riches and comfort? Cato promised his soldiers the figs of Africa, Caesar promised his the riches of Gaul, and, for better or worse, the soldiers followed them. But you're promising poverty and persecution. Who do you think's going to follow you?" You went ahead unafraid, and I can hear you saying you were the grain of wheat that must die before it bears fruit; and that you must be raised upon a cross and from there draw the whole world up to you.

Today, this has happened: they raised you up on a cross. You took advantage of that to hold out your arms and draw people up to you. And countless people have come to the foot of the cross, to fling themselves into your arms.

✳ JOHN PAUL I (1912–78)

85
Finding Ourselves

When we find the truth that shapes our lives we have found more than an idea. We have found a Person. We have come upon the actions of One Who is still hidden, but Whose work proclaims Him holy and worthy to be adored. And in Him we also find ourselves.

✳ THOMAS MERTON (1915–68)

86

Seeing Christ Everywhere

In order to face suffering in peace: suffer without imposing on others a theory of suffering, . . . without proclaiming yourself a martyr, without counting out the price of your courage, without disdaining sympathy, and without seeking too much of it.

We must be sincere in our sufferings as in anything else. We must recognize at once our weakness and our pain, but we do not need to advertise them. We must face the fact that it is much harder to stand the long monotony of slight suffering than a passing onslaught of intense pain.

In either case, what is hard is our own poverty, and the spectacle of our own selves reduced more and more to nothing, wasting away in our own estimation and in that of our friends. We must be willing to accept also the bitter truth that, in the end, we may have to become a burden to those who love us.

But it is necessary that we face this also. It takes heroic charity and humility to let others sustain us when we are absolutely incapable of sustaining ourselves.

We cannot suffer well unless we see Christ everywhere—both in suffering and in the charity of those who come to the aid of our affliction.

✳ THOMAS MERTON (1915–68)

87

A Bishop Will Die

I have often been threatened with death. I have to say, as a Christian, that I don't believe in death without resurrection: if they kill me, I will rise again in the Salvadoran people. I tell you this without any boasting, with the greatest humility. As pastor, I am obliged, by divine command, to give my life for those I love, who are all Salvadorans, even for those who are going to assassinate me. If the threats are carried out, even now I offer my blood to God for the redemption and resurrection of El Salvador. Martyrdom is a grace of God I don't think I deserve. But if God accepts the sacrifice of my life, may my blood be the seed of liberty and the sign that hope will soon become reality. May my death, if accepted by God, be for the freedom of my people and as a witness to hope in the future. You can say, if they come to kill me, that I forgive and bless those who do it. Hopefully they may realize that they will be wasting their time. A bishop will die, but the Church of God, which is the people, will never perish.

✳ OSCAR ROMERO (1917–80)

88

Peace

Peace is not the product of terror or fear.

Peace is not the silence of cemeteries.

Peace is not the silent result of violent repression.

Peace is the generous, tranquil contribution of all to the
good of all.

Peace is dynamism. Peace is generosity.

It is right and it is duty.

✳ OSCAR ROMERO (1917–80)

89

Quick to Learn, Slow to Condemn

More than anyone else, Christians ought to feel the obligation to conform their conscience to the truth. Before the splendor of the free gift of God's revelation in Christ, how humbly and attentively must we listen to the voice of conscience. How modest must we be in regard to our own limited insight. How quick must we be to learn and how slow to condemn. One of the constant temptations in every age, even among Christians, is to make oneself the norm of truth. In an age of pervasive individualism, this temptation takes a variety of forms. But the mark of those who are in the truth is the ability to love humbly. This is what Jesus teaches us: truth is expressed in love.

✳ JOHN PAUL II (B. 1920)

90
Witnesses of Hope

We are witnesses. Witnesses of a shining faith; of an active, patient, and kindly charity; of a service for the many forms of poverty experienced by contemporary humanity. Witnesses of the hope that does not disappoint and of the deep communion that reflects the life of God, of the Trinity, of obedience and the cross. In short, witnesses of holiness, people of the Beatitudes, called to be perfect as the heavenly Father is perfect.

✳ JOHN PAUL II (B. 1920)

91
What Faith Demands

How can we profess faith in God's Word, and then refuse to let it inspire and direct our thinking, our activity, our decisions, and our responsibilities toward one another? Faith is always demanding, because faith leads us beyond ourselves. Faith imparts a vision of life's purpose and stimulates us to action.

✳ JOHN PAUL II (B. 1920)

92

The Law Written in the Heart

We do not live in an irrational or meaningless world. On the contrary, there is a moral logic that is built into human life. We must find a way to discuss the human future intelligibly. The universal moral law written on the human heart is precisely that kind of "grammar" which is needed if the world is to engage in this discussion of its future. The politics of nations can never ignore the transcendent, spiritual dimension of the human experience.

✷ JOHN PAUL II (B. 1920)

93
Forgiveness and Justice

An essential prerequisite for forgiveness and reconciliation is justice, which finds its ultimate foundation in the law of God and in His plan of love and mercy for humanity. Understood in this way, justice is not limited to establishing what is right between the parties in conflict but looks above all to reestablishing authentic relationships with God, with oneself, and with others. Thus there is no contradiction between forgiveness and justice. Forgiveness neither eliminates nor lessens the need for the reparation which justice requires, but seeks to reintegrate individuals and groups into society, and states into the community of nations. No punishment can suppress the inalienable dignity of those who have committed evil. The door to repentance and rehabilitation must always remain open.

✳ JOHN PAUL II (B. 1920)

94
Finding a Second Childhood

Many of us, who want to offer consolation, experience deep inner desolation. Many of us, who want to offer healing and affection to others, experience a seemingly inexhaustible hunger for intimacy. Many of us, who speak to others about the beauty of family life, friendship, and community, come home at night to a place that feels more like an empty cave than a true home. Many of us, who let water flow on the heads of those who search for a new family, give bread to those who search for a new community, and touch with oil those who search for healing, find ourselves with dry, hungry, and sick hearts, restless during the day and anxious during the night. Yes, indeed, many of us have lost touch with our identity as children of God.

But it is precisely this childhood that Mary wants us to claim. She, who offered an immaculate space for God to take on human flesh, wants to offer us also a space where we can be reborn as Jesus was born. With the same heart that she loved Jesus, she wants to love us. It is a heart that will not make us wonder anxiously whether we are truly loved. It is a heart that has not been marked by the infidelities of the human race and so will never bring wounds to those who seek peace there. Jesus has given her to us so that she could guide us in our search for a second childhood, assist us as we try to shake off our sadness, and open the way to true inner peace.

✳ HENRI J. M. NOUWEN (1932–96)

95
To Love Deeply

D o not hesitate to love and to love deeply. You might be afraid of the pain that deep love can cause. When those you love deeply reject you, leave you, or die, your heart will be broken. But that should not hold you back from loving deeply. The pain that comes from deep love makes your love ever more fruitful. It is like a plow that breaks the ground to allow the seed to take root and grow into a strong plant. Every time you experience the pain of rejection, absence, or death, you are faced with a choice. You can become bitter and decide not to love again, or you can stand straight in your pain and let the soil on which you stand become richer and more able to give life to new seeds.

The more you have loved and have allowed yourself to suffer because of your love, the more you will be able to let your heart grow wider and deeper. When your love is truly giving and receiving, those whom you love will not leave your heart even when they depart from you. They will become part of your self and thus gradually build a community within you. . . . Yes, as you love deeply the ground of your heart will be broken more and more, but you will rejoice in the abundance of the fruit it will bear.

✳ HENRI J. M. NOUWEN (1932–96)

96
Child of God

The truth, even though I cannot feel it right now, is that I am the chosen child of God, precious in God's eyes, called the Beloved from all eternity and held safe in an everlasting embrace. . . . We must dare to opt consciously for our chosenness and not allow our emotions, feelings, or passions to seduce us into self-rejection.

✴ HENRI J. M. NOUWEN (1932–96)

97

To Wait Open-Endedly

To wait open-endedly is an enormously radical attitude toward life. So is to trust that something will happen to us that is far beyond our imaginings. So, too, is giving up control over our future and letting God define our life, trusting that God molds us according to God's love and not according to our fear. The spiritual life is a life in which we wait, actively present to the moment, trusting that new things will happen to us, new things that are far beyond our own imagination, fantasy, or prediction. That, indeed, is a very radical stance toward life in a world preoccupied with control.

✳ HENRI J. M. NOUWEN (1932–96)

98

If You Really Want to Know God

I f you really want to know God, go to his people. Go to your barber and talk about God. Tell the carpenter about what you're experiencing. Take time to read the lives of the saints. They always knock you off your feet because they tell you the preoccupations you have aren't the ones you should have. Get in touch with those women and men who did crazy things like falling in love with God.

✳ Henri J. M. Nouwen (1932–96)

99

Dare to Love

D are to love and to be a real friend. The love you give and receive is a reality that will lead you closer and closer to God as well as to those whom God has given you to love.

✳ HENRI J. M. NOUWEN (1932–96)

100
Final Words

As I write these final words, my heart is filled with joy. I am at peace.

It is the first day of November, and fall is giving way to winter. Soon the trees will lose the vibrant colors of their leaves and snow will cover the ground. The earth will shut down, and people will race to and from their destinations bundled up for warmth. Chicago winters are harsh. It is a time of dying. But we know that spring will soon come with all its new life and wonder.

It is quite clear that I will not be alive in the spring. But I will soon experience new life in a different way. Although I do not know what to expect in the afterlife, I do know that just as God has called me to serve him to the best of my abilities throughout my life on earth, he is now calling me home.

✳ JOSEPH BERNARDIN (1928–96)

Authors

✳ ANDREW OF CRETE (CA. 660–740). Theologian. Reputed to have invented the canon as a musical form: #11, #12.

✳ ANTOINE FRÉDÉRIC OZANAM (1813–53). French scholar and founder of the Society of St. Vincent de Paul: #50.

✳ AUGUSTINE OF HIPPO (354–430). Bishop of Hippo in North Africa. Theologian and monastic founder. Doctor of the church: #6, #7.

✳ BASIL THE GREAT (CA. 330–79). Cappadocian Father. Bishop of Caesarea from 370. Doctor of the church: #3.

✳ BEDE GRIFFITHS (1906–93). English Benedictine monk. In India, became known as a bridge between East and West: #75.

✳ BERNARD OF CLAIRVAUX (1090–1153). French Cistercian abbot who exercised immense influence. Doctor of the church: #13.

✳ BROTHER LAWRENCE (1614–91). French Carmelite lay brother and mystic: #45.

✳ CAESARIUS OF ARLES (CA. 470–542). Monk of the island of Lerins. Archbishop of Arles at the age of thirty-three: #9.

✳ CARLO CARRETTO (1910–88). Italian youth leader who subsequently became a priest and a follower of Charles de Foucauld: #79.

✳ CATHERINE OF SIENA (CA. 1347–80). Influential Italian Dominican tertiary and mystic. Doctor of the church: #26.

✳ CHARLES DE FOUCAULD (1858–1916). French soldier and mystic, known as the "Hermit of the Sahara." Inspired the formation of the Little Brothers of Jesus and the Little Sisters of Jesus: #55.

✳ *THE CLOUD OF UNKNOWING* (FOURTEENTH CENTURY). Anonymous contemplative work: #24.

✳ COLUMBANUS (CA. 543–615). Irish missionary. Worked in France, Germany, and Italy: #10.

✳ DANTE ALIGHIERI (1265–1321). Italian poet and philosopher. Author of *The Divine Comedy*: #22, #23.

✳ DOROTHY DAY (1897–1980). Prominent American pacifist, journalist, and social activist: #70, #71, #72.

✳ FRANCIS DE SALES (1567–1622). Bishop of Geneva from 1602. Cofounder of the Visitation Order: #40, #41.

✳ FRANCIS OF ASSISI (CA. 1181–1226). Founder of the Franciscans (1209). Deeply committed to the poor: #17, #18.

✳ FULTON SHEEN (1895–1979). American archbishop. Popular writer, preacher, and radio and television speaker: #68, #69.

✳ GERARD MANLEY HOPKINS (1844–89). English Jesuit poet and professor of Greek in Dublin: #51, #52, #53, #54.

✳ HENRI J. M. NOUWEN (1932–96). Dutch American priest, writer, teacher, and spiritual director: #94, #95, #96, #97, #98.

✳ HILDEGARD OF BINGEN (1098–1179). German mystic and Benedictine abbess: #15, #16, #17.

✳ IGNATIUS OF LOYOLA (1491–1556). Spanish soldier. Founder of the Society of Jesus (1540): #30, #31, #32.

✳ JEAN-PIERRE DE CAUSSADE (1675–1751). French Jesuit known for his book *Self-Abandonment to Divine Providence:* #47.

✳ JOHN CHAPMAN (1865–1933). English Benedictine monk and author. Abbot of Downside from 1929: #56.

✳ JOHN CHRYSOSTOM (CA. 349–407). Patriarch of Constantinople whose last name means "golden mouth." Doctor of the church: #4, #5.

✳ JOHN HENRY NEWMAN (1801–90). Established the Oratorians in England (1849). Cardinal from 1879–90: #48, #49.

✳ JOHN OF THE CROSS (1542–91). Spanish mystic and co-reformer of the Discalced Carmelites. Doctor of the church: #37, #38.

✳ JOHN PAUL I (1912–78). Pope from August 26 to September 28, 1978: #84.

✳ JOHN PAUL II (B. 1920). Pope from 1978 to the present: #89, #90, #91, #92, #93.

✳ JOSEPH BERNARDIN (1928–96). Cardinal archbishop of Chicago. Recipient of the Medal of Freedom in 1996: #100.

✳ JULIAN OF NORWICH (CA. 1342–CA. 1420). English anchoress and spiritual writer: #25.

✳ KARL RAHNER (1904–84). Influential German Jesuit theologian. Prominent at the Second Vatican Council: #73, #74.

✳ MARGARET MARY ALACOQUE (1647–90). French Visitandine nun and promoter of devotion to the Sacred Heart: #46.

✳ MATTEO RICCI (1552–1610). One of the first Jesuits. Journeyed to the Orient: #39.

✳ MOTHER TERESA (1910–97). Born of an Albanian family in Skopje (Macedonia). Founder of the Missionaries of Charity (1949): #80, #81, #82, #83.

✳ OSCAR ROMERO (1917–80). Archbishop of San Salvador from 1977. Murdered while celebrating Mass in his diocese: #87, #88.

✳ PADRE PIO (1887–1968). Italian Franciscan priest and mystic: #66, #67.

✳ PATRICK (CA. 390–CA. 461). "Apostle to the Irish": #8.

✳ PAUL (CA. 10–CA. 67) Writer, teacher, and early disciple who spread the teachings of Jesus Christ to Jews and Gentiles throughout the Mediterranean world: #1, #2.

✳ PEDRO ARRUPE (1907–91). Basque superior general of the Jesuits (1965–83). Ministered to atomic-bomb victims at Hiroshima in 1945: #76, #77, #78.

✳ PETER CANISIUS (1521–97). Jesuit priest and inspired leader of the Catholic Reformation: #35.

✳ PETER FAVRE (1506–46). French farm boy who became friend of St. Ignatius of Loyola and roomed with Francis Xavier. Became first Jesuit: #33.

✳ PIERRE TEILHARD DE CHARDIN (1881–1955). French Jesuit theologian and scientist: #61, #62, #63, #64, #65.

✳ ROBERT BELLARMINE (1542–1621). Italian Jesuit priest, author, and theologian to two popes: #36.

✳ ROSE OF LIMA (1586–1617). Peruvian of Spanish origin. Dominican tertiary: #44.

✳ TERESA OF ÁVILA (1515–82). Spanish mystic and co-reformer of the Discalced Carmelites. Doctor of the church: #34.

✳ THÉRÈSE OF LISIEUX (1873–97). French Carmelite. A patron saint of France. Doctor of the church: #57, #58, #59, #60.

✳ THOMAS À KEMPIS (CA. 1380–1471). Dutch Augustinian canon. Author of *The Imitation of Christ*: #27, #28, #29.

✳ THOMAS AQUINAS (CA. 1225–74). Italian Dominican philosopher and theologian. Doctor of the church: #19, #20, #21.

✳ THOMAS MERTON (1915–68). Influential American Cistercian monk and writer: #85, #86.

✳ VINCENT DE PAUL (CA. 1580–1660). French servant of the poor. Founded the Sisters of Charity and the Congregation of the Mission (Vincentians): #42, #43.

Sources

Paul: Philippians 2 and Romans 8:38–39. New Revised Standard Version Bible: Catholic Edition (Oxford University Press, 1989).

Basil the Great: From the treatise "On the Holy Spirit," chapter 9.

John Chrysostom: From the homilies of St. John Chrysostom, homily 50.3.4.

Augustine of Hippo: The Confessions of St. Augustine, translated by Maria Boulding (London: Hodder, 1997); *The City of God,* translated by Maria Boulding (London: Hodder, 1997).

Patrick: Voices of the Saints, Bert Ghezzi (New York: Doubleday, 2000).

Caesarius of Arles: From the sermons of St. Caesarius of Arles, sermon 25.1.

Columbanus: Instruction 1 on Faith, "Sancti Columbani Opera."

Andrew of Crete: From Homily Or. 10.

Bernard of Clairvaux: A reading from the sermons of St. Bernard, De diversis 5:4–5.

Hildegard of Bingen: Hildegard of Bingen: An Anthology, translated by Robert Carver, edited by Fiona Bowie and Oliver Davies (London: SPCK, 1990).

Francis of Assisi: Francis and Clare: The Complete Works, translated by Regis J. Armstrong and Ignatius C. Brady, Classics of Western Spirituality (New York: Paulist Press, 1982); *Francis of Assisi: Early Documents,* vol. I, *The Saint,* edited by Regis J. Armstrong, O.F.M. Cap.; J. A. Wayne Hellmann, O.F.M. Conv.; and William J. Short, O.F.M. (London, New York, and the Philippines: New City Press). © 1999 Franciscan Institute of St. Bonaventure, New York.

Thomas Aquinas: Sermon on the Apostles Creed 13–14. English translation in *The Three Greatest Prayers* (Westminster, Md.: Newman Press, 1956); *Summa Theologica.*

Dante Alighieri: Inferno, translated by Dorothy L. Sayers (London: David Higham Associates, 1947); *Paradiso,* translated by Mark Musa (Bloomington, IN: Indiana University Press, 1984).

The Cloud of Unknowing: Edited by James Walsh, S.J., Classics of Western Spirituality (New York: Paulist Press, 1981).

Julian of Norwich: Revelations of Divine Love, chapters 5 and 86, taken from *All Shall Be Well* by Sheila Upjohn (London: Darton, Longman and Todd, 1992).

Catherine of Siena: The Dialogue, translated by Suzanne Noffke, Classics of Western Spirituality (New York: Paulist Press, 1980).

Thomas à Kempis: The Imitation of Christ, translated by Ronald Knox and Michael Oakley (London: Burns and Oates, 1959).

Ignatius of Loyola: The Spiritual Exercises of St. Ignatius, translated by Louis J. Puhl (Chicago: Loyola University Press, 1951); *Hearts on Fire: Praying with Jesuits,* collected and edited by Michael Harter, S.J. (St. Louis: Institute of Jesuit Sources, 1993).

Peter Favre: The Spiritual Writings of Pierre Favre (St. Louis: Institute of Jesuit Sources, 1996).

Teresa of Ávila: The Way of Perfectio (original source). This translation from *Living Water: Daily Readings with St. Teresa of Ávila,* edited by Sister Mary, O.D.C. (London: Darton, Longman and Todd, 1986).

Peter Canisius: Voices of the Saints, Bert Ghezzi (New York: Doubleday, 2000).

Robert Bellarmine: Voices of the Saints, Bert Ghezzi (New York: Doubleday, 2000).

John of the Cross: Centered on Love: The Poems of St. John of the Cross, translated by Marjorie Flower, O.C.D. (© 1983 The Carmelite Community, St. Andrew's Road, Varroville, NSW 2565, Australia), quoted by Iain Matthew, O.C.D., in *The Impact of God*

(London: Hodder, 1995); *Dark Night of the Soul,* translated by Marjorie Flower, O.C.D. © 1983 in *Poems of St. John of the Cross* (published by the Carmelite Community, St. Andrew's Road, Varroville, NSW 2565 Australia), reproduced in *The Impact of God,* by Iain Matthew, O.C.D. (London: Hodder, 1995).

Matteo Ricci: The True Meaning of the Lord of Heaven (St. Louis: Institute of Jesuit Sources, 1985).

Francis de Sales: A Thirst for God: Daily Readings with St. Francis de Sales, edited by Michael Hollings (London: Darton, Longman and Todd, 1985).

Vincent de Paul: From the writings of St. Vincent de Paul.

Rose of Lima: From the writings of St. Rose of Lima.

Brother Lawrence: An Oratory of the Heart: Daily Readings with Brother Lawrence of the Resurrection, arranged and introduced by Robert Llewelyn (London: Darton, Longman and Todd, 1984).

Margaret Mary Alocoque: Voices of the Saints, Bert Ghezzi (New York: Doubleday, 2000).

Jean-Pierre de Caussade: The Sacrament of the Present Moment, translated by Kitty Muggeridge (New York: HarperCollins, 1981).

John Henry Newman: English Spiritual Writers (New York: Sheed & Ward, 1962).

Antoine Frédéric Ozanam: From a letter to Father Pendola, July 19, 1853. Reproduced in *Through the Eye of a Needle* by Frédéric Ozanam (Strathfield: St. Pauls, 1989).

Gerard Manley Hopkins: Hearts on Fire: Praying with Jesuits, collected and edited by Michael Harter, S.J. (St. Louis: Institute of Jesuit Sources, 1993).

Charles de Foucald: The Catholic Prayer Book, compiled by Monsignor Michael Buckley and edited by Tony Castle (Ann Arbor, MI: Servant Publications, 1986).

John Chapman: From *Spiritual Letters,* 2nd ed. (London: Sheed and Ward, 1935).

Thérèse of Lisieux: Autobiography of St. Thérèse of Lisieux (original source). Taken from *By Love Alone: Daily Readings with St. Thérèse of Lisieux,* edited by Michael Hollings (London: Darton, Longman and Todd, 1986).

Pierre Teilhard de Chardin: From *Hymn of the Universe,* by Pierre Teilhard de Chardin, English translation (New York: Harper and Row, 1965). © Georges Borchardt, Inc.; *Hearts on Fire: Praying with*

Jesuits, collected and edited by Michael Harter, S.J. (St. Louis: Institute of Jesuit Sources, 1993).

Padre Pio: From letter of Passion Sunday, March 29, 1914, to Raffaelina Cerase, taken from *Correspondence,* vol. 2 (Editions "Padre Pio da Pietrelcina," 71013 San Giovanni Rotondo, Italy, 1997).

Fulton Sheen. From *Lift Up Your Heart*, by Fulton Sheen (London: Burns and Oates, 1950); *Go to Heaven* (New York: McGraw-Hill, 1960).

Dorothy Day: Dorothy Day, Selected Writings: By Little and by Little, edited by Robert Ellsberg (Maryknoll, NY: Orbis Books, 1992); *The Long Loneliness: The Autobiography of Dorothy Day* (San Francisco: Harper and Row, 1952); *On Pilgrimage: The Sixties* and *From Union Square to Rome,* by Dorothy Day (Silver Spring, MD: Preservation of the Faith Press, 1938).

Karl Rahner: From *The Eternal Year* (London: Burns and Oates, 1964).

Bede Griffiths. From "Prayer," a talk at Kreuth, Germany, April 7, 1992, reproduced in *Beyond the Darkness: A Biography of Bede Griffiths,* by Shirley du Boulay (London: Rider, 1998).

Pedro Arrupe: Hearts on Fire: Praying with Jesuits, collected and edited by Michael Harter, S.J. (St. Louis: Institute of Jesuit Sources, 1993) and *One Jesuit's Spiritual Journey: Autobiographical Conversations with Jean-Claude Dietsch* (St. Louis: Institute of Jesuit Sources, 1986).

Carlo Carretto: God of the Impossible: Daily Readings with Carlo Carretto (London: Darton, Longman and Todd, 1988).

Mother Teresa: No Greater Love, edited by Joseph Durepos (Novato, CA: New World Library, 1997).

John Paul I: Illustrissimi: The Letters of Pope John Paul I (London: Collins, 1978).

Thomas Merton: No Man Is an Island (London: Burns and Oates, 1955); *The Shining Wilderness: Daily Readings with Thomas Merton* (London: Darton, Longman and Todd, 1988).

Oscar Romero: Homilías, vol. 4, May 11, 1978.

John Paul II: Go in Peace, edited by Joseph Durepos (Chicago: Loyola Press, 2003).

Henri J. M. Nouwen: The Inner Voice of Love (London: Darton, Longman and Todd, 1996) and excerpts taken from several addresses delivered in Toronto.

Joseph Bernardin: The Gift of Peace: Personal Reflections by Cardinal Joseph Bernardin (Chicago: Loyola Press, 1996).

Index of Authors